EVERY DAY

ALTERATIONS

A Compendium of Causes, Effects
and Remedies for the more
Common Errors in Cutting
and Making Men's
Garments

By

Jno. A. Carlstrom

British Library Cataloguing-in-Publication Data
A catalogue record for this book is available from
the British Library

Dressmaking and Tailoring

Dressmaking and Tailoring broadly refers to those who make, repair or alter clothing for a profession. A dressmaker will traditionally make custom clothing for women, ranging from dresses and blouses to full evening gowns (also historically called a mantua-maker or a modiste). Whereas a tailor will do the same, but usually for men's clothing - especially suits. The terms essentially refer to a specific set of hand and machine sewing skills, as well as pressing techniques that are unique to the construction of traditional clothing. This is separate to 'made to measure', which uses a set of pre-existing patterns. Usually, a bespoke tailored suit or dress will be completely original and unique to the customer, and hence such items have been highly desirable since the trade first appeared in the thirteenth century. The Oxford English Dictionary states that the word 'tailor' first came into usage around the 1290s, and undoubtedly by this point, tailoring guilds, as well as those of cloth merchants and weavers were well established across Europe.

As the tailoring profession has evolved, so too have the methods of tailoring. There are a number of distinctive business models which modern tailors may practice, such as 'local tailoring' where the tailor is met locally, and the garment is produced locally too, 'distance tailoring', where a garment is ordered from an out-of-town tailor, enabling cheaper labour to be used -

which, in practice can now be done on a global scale via e-commerce websites, and a 'travelling tailor', where the man or woman will travel between cities, usually stationing in a luxury hotel to provide the client the same tailoring services they would provide in their local store. These processes are the same for both women's and men's garment making.

Pattern making is a very important part of this profession; the construction of a paper or cardboard template from which the parts of a garment are traced onto fabric before cutting our and assembling. A custom dressmaker (or tailor) frequently employs one of three pattern creation methods; a 'flat-pattern method' which begins with the creation of a sloper or block (a basic pattern for a garment, made to the wearer's measurements), which can then be used to create patterns for many styles of garments, with varying necklines, sleeves, dart placements and so on. Although it is also used for womenswear, the 'drafting method' is more commonly employed in menswear and involves drafting a pattern directly onto pattern paper using a variety of straightedges and curves. Since menswear rarely involves draping, pattern-making is the primary preparation for creating a cut-and-sew woven garment. The third method, the 'pattern draping method' is used when the patternmaker's skill is not matched with the difficulty of the design. It involves creating a muslin mock-up pattern, by pinning fabric directly on a dress form, then transferring the muslin outline and markings onto a paper pattern or using the muslin as the pattern itself.

Dressmaking and tailoring has become a very well respected profession; dressmakers such as Pierre Balmain, Christian Dior, Cristóbal Balenciaga and Coco Chanel have gone on to achieve international acclaim and fashion notoriety. Balmain, known for sophistication and elegance, once said that 'dressmaking is the architecture of movement.' Whilst tailors, due to the nature of their profession - catering to men's fashions, have not garnered such levels of individual fame, areas such as 'Savile Row' in the United Kingdom are today seen as the heart of the trade.

TWO VIEWS

Alterations

The Cutter's View.

The gods gave to the cutter
  The system, taste and wit,
On wings of art to flutter
  And always make a fit;
But the devil rules the making,
  And very sad to tell,
Alt'rations sure are breaking
  Into profits to beat ——!

Busheling

The Tailor's View.

The tailor is the moulder
  Of all the form and grace
That clothes possess, in shoulder,
  Lapel and every place.
If it wasn't for the cutter,
  Who hacks and chops and kills
You'd scarcely speak or utter
  A word of busheling bills.

——— :: ———

INDEX

COATS

SLEEVES

VESTS

TROUSERS

INTRODUCTION

ONE OF the interesting things about tailoring is that it constantly furnishes problems for solution. After we have acquired all the knowledge possible of how to cut garments and superintend their making, which are the two principal factors in producing good garments, we find that a certain percentage of the output requires some major or minor alterations. The smaller the percentage the better the cutter, but let us hope the day will never come when the public will take so little interest in what they wear that no alterations will be needed. So long as there is alteration there will be tailoring and so long as there is tailoring there will be alterations. Some trades require more and others less, and the higher the grade and the more fastidious the patronage the higher the percentage of alterations.

Regardless of how much or how little alterations are needed, the skill with which they are performed is an asset to any firm, since the object of making garments is not to merely go through a certain process and not only to satisfy a customer, but to maintain a high standard of that product. Most alterations, even the large ones that are made by good houses, are done without the request coming from the customer. It is good business policy to make them whenever the occasion demands it.

A skillful alteration that perfects a faulty garment is money and time well spent, because it is always cheaper to alter a garment than to make a new one and to satisfy a customer is the only way to hold him. To satisfy a customer means more than to avoid an alteration if he does not request it. A bungling, makeshift alteration is always expensive, because the difference between the time spent in making a halfway and a complete alteration is small, while the effect is large. Therefore, no matter how viewed, the art of altering is an important one. This is recognized by all who aim to "make good," yet, strange to say, it is one of the features that textbook publishers who cater to tailoring have overlooked and this volume enters a field that it, therefore, occupies alone, and we believe it will fill a long felt want.

Though it is impossible to cover all of the alterations that come up in actual practice and as many occur but rarely, the illustrations and descriptions have been held down to the important ones and will be found direct, as well as completely analytic of the cause, or causes, that bring them about in both cutting and making.

Believing that anything that contributes to the trades' increased knowledge is valuable, these pages, which are the result of a large experience, are submitted for the trades' approval.

WRINKLES UNDER THE BACK OF THE COLLAR

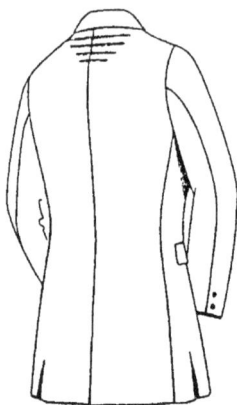

Sketch 1.

THE CAUSE of this familiar fault is usually put down as the result of the backpart-shoulder seam being too long from the end of the shoulder to the neck, or too much length of the backpart at the top, and it is therefore considered a fault in cutting.

Though this is true in a general sense, it is often caused by other reasons than cutting too long a shoulder seam, or too long a backpart at the point affected. It is frequently produced in making and from more than one cause. A short collar will always produce it. The backpart held too full to the forepart, near the neck, in joining the shoulder seam is another reason. Linings short at that point will give it and even too narrow a lining will affect it the same way.

Therefore, no set rule can be given as a remedy until the case is analyzed and the cause is located. To let the back up will ordinarily remedy the defect, because if the backpart is too long, that will shorten it. If the collar is too short, that will narrow the top to correspond to the width of collar available. If the linings are short or narrow, the outside will be adjusted to it. If the front canvases are out of adjustment the opening of the shoulder gives the opportunity to rectify it.

All of this can be done without knowing the reason for it, but as this will not prevent its recurrence the cause should be ascertained in each instance. When we know the reason for anything we approach the problem intelligently and the remedy suggests itself. To let the fullness up, if it is needed over the blades, is not a remedy, but merely "Borrowing from Peter to pay Paul." To place too much of the backpart fullness near the collar on the shoulder seam is not a good plan at any time. It is one of the remnants left of the days when the concave shoulder was the proper effect, but which is not in vogue today and therefore cannot be applied without giving the effect shown in the sketch, since the shoulder is both cut and worked differently.

Fullness placed near the end of the shoulder will give blade room and incidentally turn the shoulder seam toward the front, thereby lifting and cleaning the back of the scye and incidentally give the required room for spring at the front of the shoulder. It goes without saying, that if fullness is placed toward the end of the shoulder instead of near the collar the tendency for wrinkles at the point illustrated would be removed from that cause and it is one of the most frequent reasons for the fault. However, ascertain the cause and alter fundamentally, according to the reason of the cause.

WRINKLES BACK OF THE SCYE

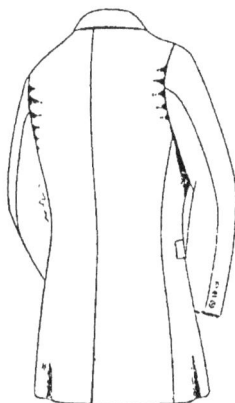

Sketch 2

THIS fault is one of the most annoying and, frequently, difficult to overcome, since it seldom originates at the point where it shows. From a cutting point of view it is created by too much shortness at the center seam. Shortness at one point always means length at another, and a short back-center seam naturally means length directly opposite, as at the points indicated.

The same fault, however, can be developed in making, even when the length quantities at the back-center seam and at the back of the scye are cut in perfect adjustment. If the shoulder is not properly "held up" at the end, by working it forward for ease at the front of the shoulder, that ease will find its way to the back and manifest itself in the same way as if it had been cut with a short back-center seam.

To illustrate this in detail the following diagrams are introduced:

Diagram 3 is the backpart as regularly drafted.

Diagram 4 shows the same backpart, of which the normal lines are shown in the light, broken lines and a straight back-center seam in the solid one. As a straight line is shorter than a curved one the solid line does not give room enough over the blades and the shortness at this point makes fullness at the back of the scye. Even when the width is made up, back of the scye, as from the broken to the solid line, not only does the material not fall into the proper position, but the run of the back-scye fails to fall evenly into the scye of the forepart.

Diagram 5 shows how to gain additional length, beyond the amount shown in the normal, in Diagram 3. The backpart may be split as shown by the broken lines, pivoting at the scye.

Diagram 6 shows the same general idea, except that it is pivoted at the back-center seam and overlapped at the scye, thereby holding the back-center seam at the normal length and making the shortness direct back of the scye. All of this refers to shortcomings caused by the cutting.

When this fault is caused by the making it is usually done by placing the fullness of the backpart shoulder too near the neck, as is shown by

Diagram 7, and very little, or none, toward the end of the shoulder. This tends to force the length, that should produce spring in front of the shoulder bone, toward the back and leave the scye portion of the forepart flat and permit the excess length to fall toward the back of the scye. The light, broken lines show the position of the backpart as cut. The heavy lines illustrate how the working leaves it.

Diagram 8 shows the proper way to work this portion of the garment

6

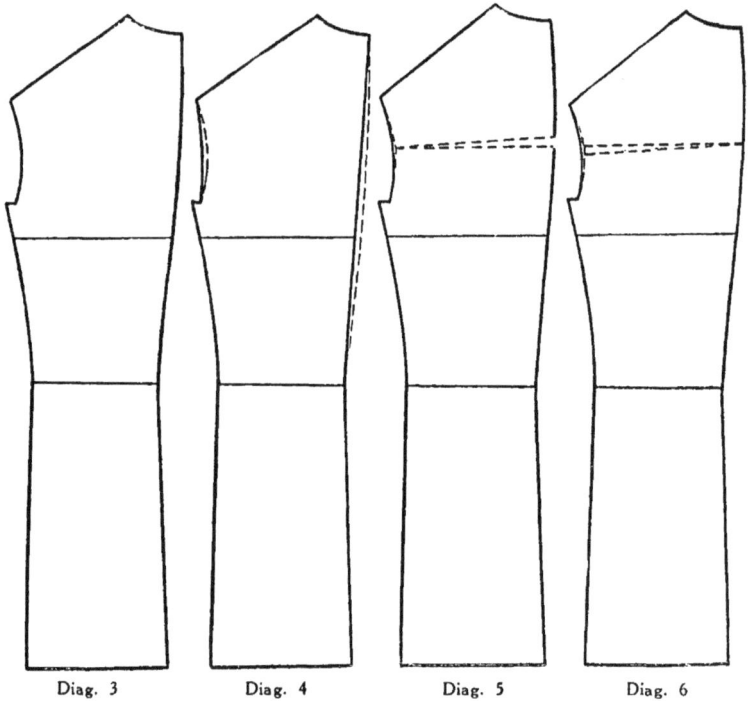

Diag. 3   Diag. 4   Diag. 5   Diag. 6

and when other details, such as the length of collar, length of linings, as well as widths, and when the canvases are placed properly, the result will be satisfactory. (Continued on Page 8.)

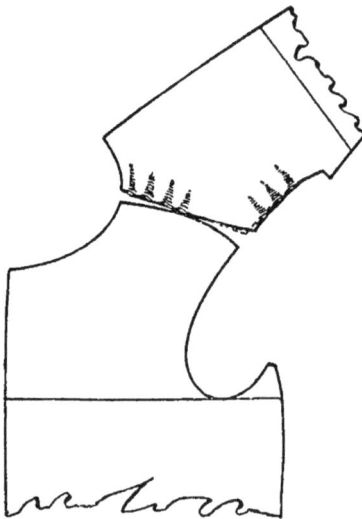

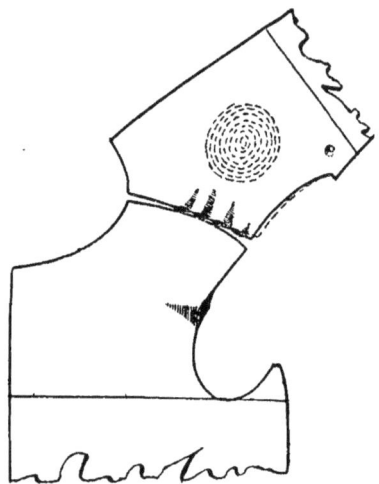

Diag. 7   Diag. 8

7

FULLNESS AT THE CREASE EDGE

Sketch 11

FROM the cutting point of view too much length at the crease edge is caused by a shoulder cut too crooked, but the fault is frequently developed by careless making. If the edge of the roll is held too tight it will naturally shorten it and cause a corresponding length at the crease edge. At other times the crease edge is stretched in making, which is easily done, since both the material and canvas are often on the bias along this line. All of these defects must be met by remedying the condition that produced it.

If the pattern is cut too crooked, and thereby causing this length, the alteration is to be made as follows:

Diagram 12 shows the pattern, as cut, by the broken lines and the solid ones show the alteration to shorten the crease edge and give more length at the front of the scye. A coat that is long at the crease edge is usually short at the front of the scye, unless the whole shoulder is too long, in which case the strap will have to be shortened, besides the changes shown. In this case the outlet at the gorge is used and the excess length is taken off at the end of the shoulder as illustrated.

BACK OF SCYE WRINKLES.

(Continued from Page 7.)

Place the fullness of the backpart shoulder seam as illustrated, in order to pocket the blade. This will curve the shoulder seam forward, as shown by the amount it falls in front of the pattern as cut, given in the broken lines. This also lifts the back of the scye and holds it clean and the surplus length falls in front of the shoulder bone, where it gives ease for the forward movements of the arm. A man should be able to move inside of his coat without disturbing it at the neck.

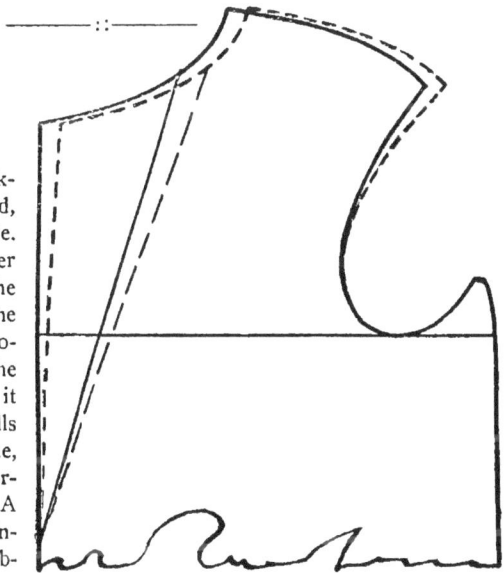

Diag. 12

FULLNESS IN FRONT OF THE SCYE

Sketch 9

THE WRINKLES in front of the scye are caused, in most instances, by cutting a too straight a shoulder. In other cases, however, it is produced in making, and the remedy should be applied with the view of correcting the fault that produced it. If the front of the scye is not held in sufficiently in making there is no use of straightening the shoulder to remedy it. The proper thing to do is to hold it in, as it should have been done in the first place. The spring that is necessary for ease at the front of the shoulder bone is, sometimes, not properly held in place, or the canvases are not properly worked and the fullness that is needed at that place is permitted to fall below the point where it belongs and shows itself as indicated by the illustration. When that is the case there is only one alteration and that is to hold in the lower part of the scye and work spring over the front bone. In other words, to give length and shortness at their proper places.

When the pattern is cut with a too straight a shoulder adjustment, the following changes are to be made:

Diagram 10 shows the pattern as cut in the broken outlines, which, by having been cut too straight causes the fault noted in Sketch 9—too much length in front of the scye. The solid outlines show the method to overcome this, by shifting the shoulder of the pattern backward, utilizing the outlet that should always be left at the end of the shoulder, or at the upper end of the scye. This will shorten the front of the scye quantity and distribute the quantities as needed. The amount the shoulder is crookened is made to correspond to the amount that it was too straight in the first place.

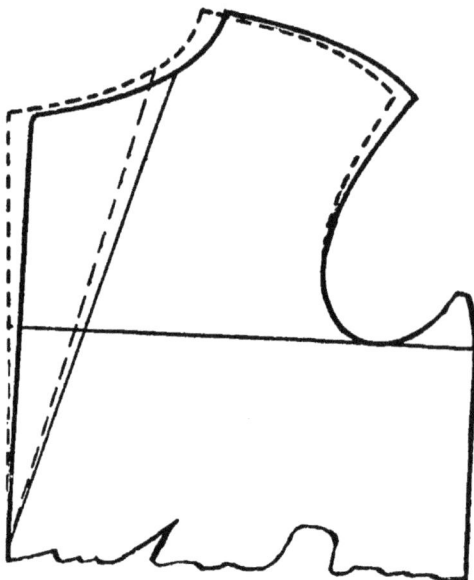

Diag. 10

9

THE FRONT-SHOULDER WRINKLE

Sketch 13

THIS is the most common and annoying defect that can occur in a garment, and is one of the faults that the trade has not yet risen above in its entirety. It is, perhaps, not one that occurs so frequently in trades where the making is above the average, as it may be set down as a fault that comes from that source practically entirely. This is in contradiction to the idea that shoulder adjustment, either a straight or a crooked shoulder, causes it, though the prevailing opinion used to be that the latter kind, in particular, was the reason. Fashion and prevailing ideas have swung from extreme straight to extreme crooked shoulders and good coats, with smooth shoulders, have been made from patterns cut during the different periods that favored each in turn.

It can be set down as a safe rule that 90 per cent of coats that break in the shoulder are faultily made. A coat cut wrong may not fit well in the shoulders, or elsewhere, but if it has wrinkles in the shoulder the fault is with the maker.

The causes that bring these wrinkles are numerous. One, that "like the poor," is always with us, is the short collar, but short canvases and linings, or lack of width of these parts will do it with equal certainty. To say to a tailor that his collar is short, or that his canvases are short, is not a convincing statement, if he does not fully understand that these parts should have excess width and length. Many figure that inasmuch as these parts go inside of the coat they require less length than the outside, while others take pride in a smooth inside for its own sake. This favors the inside at the expense of the outside and leaves the strain to show on the outside, and there is always more or less strain.

A tailor who will answer the argument that his collar is short, by stating that there is a half-inch of fullness in it, is not in position to understand the requirements. As the coat collar must fall into the offset of the linen collar and have sufficient length to stand up at the same angle above the offset, considerable length is necessary. Many good houses insist on collars having two inches of fullness, in order to get this effect.

Again, a long gorge is necessary to make smoothness, which is different from a front shoulder stretched before joining. The canvases should be made the shape required and with the proper length of collar at the gorge and the proper spring at the end of the shoulder, the outside material, which is flexible, will fall into position, if properly handled. It is useless to shape

(Continued on Page 11.)

THE BROKEN FRONT

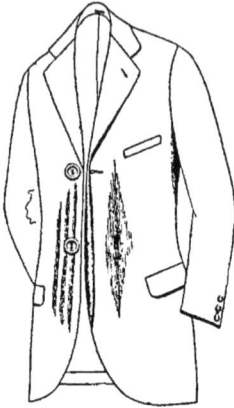

Sketch 14

ONE of the defects that does more to disfigure a garment than anything else is the broken front. It takes two forms, one of which is to turn over at the edge, as is here given in an emphasized form, for better illustration, on the left forepart, and the other the waving, perpendicular breaks on the right side. Of course, no cutting can effect this, and it must, therefore, be treated from a making point of view entirely. A long edge can be produced by a too crooked a shoulder, which has a tendency to make the lower part of the coat fall away, while an over-straight shoulder will cause overlapping at the lower button. Yet neither of these cases apply to a "rippled" front, or an over-turning edge, for no matter if the fronts overlap or fall away the broken front is no part of it unless it is put there.

The cause of the rolling front shown on the left forepart is too wide a facing and canvas and shortness, at the point where the facing and lining join, will emphasize it. The trick of the right amount of length and width is the solution. Sometimes the facing is permitted to be long on the edge, as compared with the length at the lining edge, and this will tend toward producing the effect. Often it is produced in basting the facing to the forepart, by not observing the exact position in which the facing should fall.

The "ripples" shown on the right forepart are mostly produced by a short and narrow canvas. No matter how carefully the edge is made and the facing basted, a short and narrow canvas will cause the defect shown.

The remedies for these faults suggest themselves when we know what has produced them.

———::———

THE FRONT SHOULDER WRINKLE.

(Continued from Page 10.)

the outside and expect the inside to conform to the harsher materials of which the canvases are composed.

The canvases are the frame on which the outside depends for its form and shape and the less stretching of the outside, with the view of gaining shape, the better the result.

The proper way to alter a broken shoulder is to produce ease to prevent the drag that causes it, no matter which part makes the strain.

TOO DEEP A SCYE

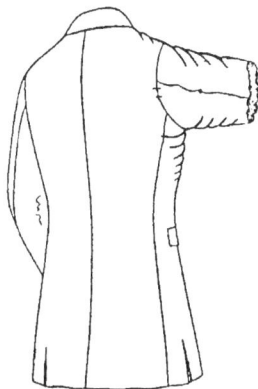

Sketch 15

ONE OF the most disfiguring ailments of a coat is a scye too deep, or cut with a run of scye that does not correspond to the part of the body where it is to fall. The coat and the sleeve may look and feel all right when the arm falls at the side of the body, but the moment the arm is raised it will produce the drags and wrinkles shown.

Sketch 15, from the back view.

Sketch 16 shows the same defect from the front view.

The reason for this is that too large an arm scye, in both depth and width, encroaches on the width of the forepart and thereby pulls from the front and at the bottom of the scye when the arm is raised.

A scye with a dug-out effect at the front holds the sleeve down when an attempt is made to raise it and causes a drag directly over the muscles, drags from the front, thereby pulling it away from the neck and, in general, causes the unsightly effect shown, besides giving a very uncomfortable feeling to the wearer.

Diagram 17 gives the outlines of the upper portion of a normal draft, showing in general the shape of the scye as it should be.

Diagram 18 shows the normal outlines, corresponding to the previous diagram in broken lines, and the heavy, solid lines that many cutters employ in shaping the scye. It is too straight over the front bone of the shoulder and has too much of a corner effect at the lower portion of the front of the scye. It is also hollowed too much below the side seam.

Diagram 19 illustrates the head of a normal sleeve and

Diagram 20 shows the same top sleeve falling evenly into the adjoining parts of the undersleeve of each part.

Diagram 21 shows a sleeve head, as often cut, in the solid lines, as compared with the normal lines shown by the broken ones.

Sketch 16.

12

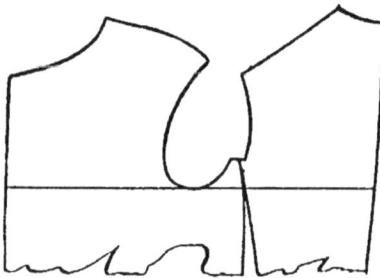

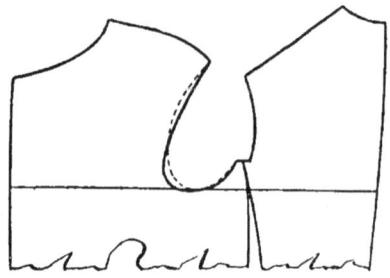

Diag. 17.   Diag. 18.

Diagram 22 shows in the solid lines how this sleeve will join, instead of as it should, as shown by the broken lines. It can easily be seen that when this sleeve, with its hollows, falling opposite the hollows of the scye of the forepart, the drags illustrated in sketches 15 and 16 are the results when the arm is raised.

Diag. 19.   Diag. 20.

The alteration for this fault is to reshape the patterns of both the forepart and the sleeve and re-cut them by the corrected patterns. At the try-on this is easily done, but on the finished garment it means more of an undertaking. Therefore, avoid wrong and uneven formations.

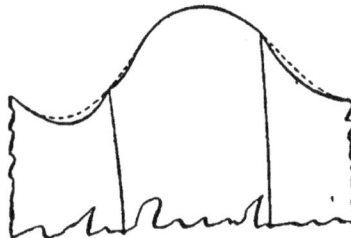

Diag. 21.   Diag. 22.

13

OVERLAPPING FRONTS

Sketch 25

WRONG balance in a garment will produce either too much or too little material at the front, which means a corresponding lack of or surplus of spring over the seat at the back. The present illustration shows too much overlap at the bottom of the front, and it follows that there is a corresponding lack of spring over the hips.

A short collar and a front edge that is held in too tight will produce the effect, and in that case require different treatment than when the balance is wrong. In fact, in each case the remedy suggests itself, for it merely means the undoing of what has been done. In cutting the cause is often wrong attitude. A normal coat cut for an erect form will throw the garment forward as far as the size at the back will permit it, at which point it will strike heavily on the hips and break over the waist, while the material at the lower button will represent all the surplus size that is otherwise evenly distributed all around the garment. Shortness infused in the making along the front edge, or at the collar, requires to be rectified at the particular points at which it appears. To alter the balance or attitude of the garment is not a satisfactory solution.

14

FRONTS SWINGING AWAY
AT BOTTOM

Sketch 26

THIS illustration shows a reverse effect of the previous one. Here we find a scarcity of materials at the front, and, as a natural consequence, there is a surplus at the back. When this fault is produced from an error in cutting it is frequently caused by cutting a normal garment for a stooping form, or in some other ways by wrong distribution of the total quantities. To remedy this requires a readjustment of the balance, which must be done by bringing the garment into place. This will disturb the shoulder section, and requires the shortening of the straps and readjustment of the gorge, which means that the collar must be taken off and the shoulders opened, which, in turn, cannot be done satisfactorily without taking the sleeves out.

A too long a strap length is one of the causes that produces this effect and requires the same alterations, in general, as already described.

These are some of the principal and frequent alterations that come up in every-day practice, and to know the cause is more than half of the remedy, because it can be handled intelligently and a large percentage avoided by repeating the same error.

15

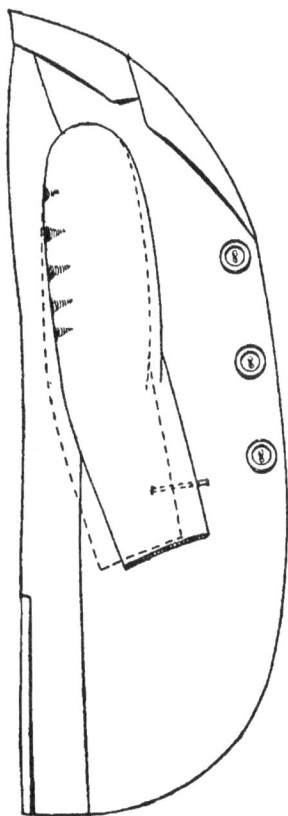

Sketch 23

ERECT COAT
NORMAL SLEEVE.

M ANY cutters give much care to their cutting and never fail to provide for the attitude in the body of the coat, but, somehow, do not feel it necessary to make the same provision for the sleeve, holding to the opinion that the attitude of the sleeve follows the body of the coat, or that it can be hung higher or lower to meet the requirement.

The present sketch illustrates an erect coat with a normal sleeve. As an erect coat falls back further than the normal the normal sleeve will fall too far forward, and to merely lower it in the scye will make the narrow part of the sleeve fall in the wide part of the scye and therefore will not make a satisfactory sleeve head.

The alteration is to cut the top of the sleeve normal, but to draw a new line as far back of the normal, at the elbow, as the degree of erectness dealt with and hold the lower part of the sleeve by this line. This will permit the sleeve to go in normally into the scye and take the same attitude as the coat from the scye downward.

16

WRONG ATTITUDE IN SLEEVES

STOOPING COAT
NORMAL SLEEVE.

THIS illustration shows the reverse of the previous diagram, or a stooping coat with a normal sleeve. As the stooping coat falls more to the front than the normal, the sleeve in normal position falls farther back than it should, as shown by the solid lines, and when the arm falls to correspond to the body it causes wrinkles at the front, as the shadings show. The broken outlines indicate where the sleeve should fall for this type, and they must be cut just the reverse to those explained for the previous diagram to have it fall to correspond to the attitude of the stooping form.

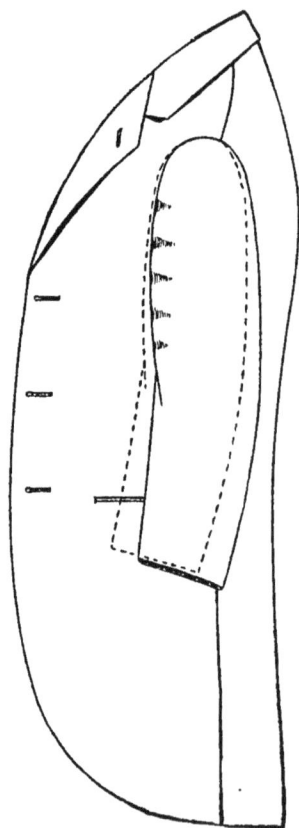

Sketch 24

ALTERATIONS ON VESTS

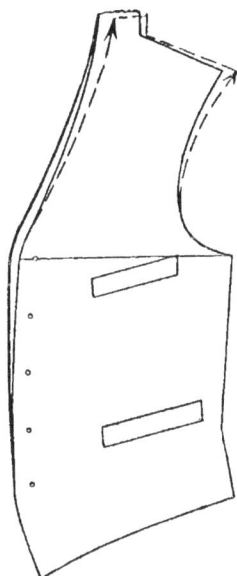

Diag. 27.

TIGHTNESS AT THE TOP BUTTON

Diagram 27 shows a frequent fault in which the garment shows a lack of size at the top button, as shown by the solid line, at which the breast line ends. The distance from it to the pannelled lines shows the amount it falls short at the top button. This makes the shoulder adjustment too straight for the size at the top button, and thereby emphasizes the lack of size at that point.

To remedy this it becomes necessary to crooken the shoulder, as shown by the broken line, ending in an arrow point. At the end of the shoulder the same amount can be let out, if the wide shoulder effect is required. In most cases it is not.

SMALLNESS AT BOTTOM OF FORE-PART.

Diagram 28 shows a lack of size at the bottom of the forepart, as from the solid to the pannelled line. The shoulder adjustment corresponds to the pannelled line, but is too crooked for the solid one. It must, therefore, be straightened, as by the broken line, ending in an arrowpoint. An outlet should always be left at this point, and in this case the shoulder can be narrowed at the scye, as by the broken line formation to the arrowpoint and across the top, as by the broken lines.

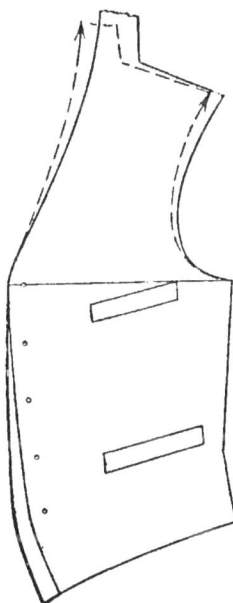

Diag. 28.

ALTERATIONS ON VESTS

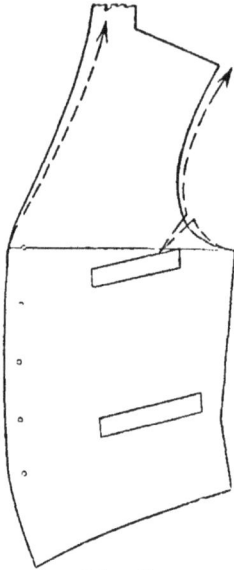

Diag. 29.

TOO MUCH FULLNESS AT SCYE

Diagram 29 illustrates too much fullness at the scye. A V taken out at this point will prove the most direct remedy, and is a frequent requirement for large-breasted men, where size is needed at the center of the forepart. The tendency to crooken the shoulder is of advantage for this type.

THE WAIST SUPPRESSION

Diagram 30. To gain chest fullness and, incidentally, a small waist effect, the V illustrated in this diagram is necessary. The amount suppressed may be more or less according to requirements. Unless an emphasized small waist effect is desired size may be added, as by the broken lines at the side seam.

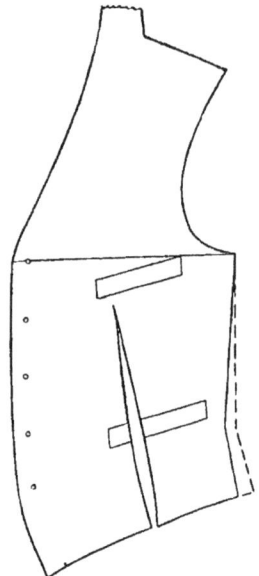

Diag. 30.

ALTERATIONS ON VESTS

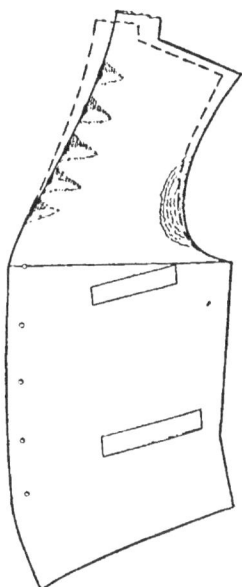

Diag. 31.

EXCESS LENGTH AT OPENING.

Diagram 31. Too much length at the opening edge is, generally speaking, when the making is not at fault, caused by too crooked a shoulder. It follows that a corresponding tightness falls at the scye. To remedy this condition is to straighten the shoulder, as is shown by the broken lines. In fact, it is considered a good thing to have the shoulder sufficiently straight so that a certain amount of fullness falls at the scye and to take that fullness out by a V, which gives chest fullness and prevents flatness that cannot fit the natural rounding found at this point.

EXCESS LENGTH AT THE SCYE

Diagram 32. When more fullness falls at the scye than can be taken out with a V, it is a case of too straight a shoulder. In that case the shoulder is to be crookened, as by the broken lines, or the reverse of the process explained in the previous diagram.

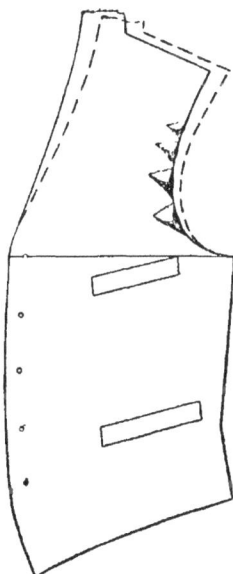

Diag. 32.

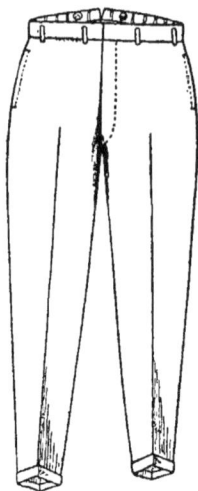

Diag. 33.

ALTERATIONS ON TROUSERS

THIS illustration shows trousers as they appear when too open in the legs. When worn they give too much length at the inseam, since the legs fall closer than the trousers, thereby forcing the material in the same direction, which strains the outside, causing shortness at that seam and corresponding length at the inseam.

Diagram 34 shows how to remedy the defect. The trousers must be opened at both seams from the

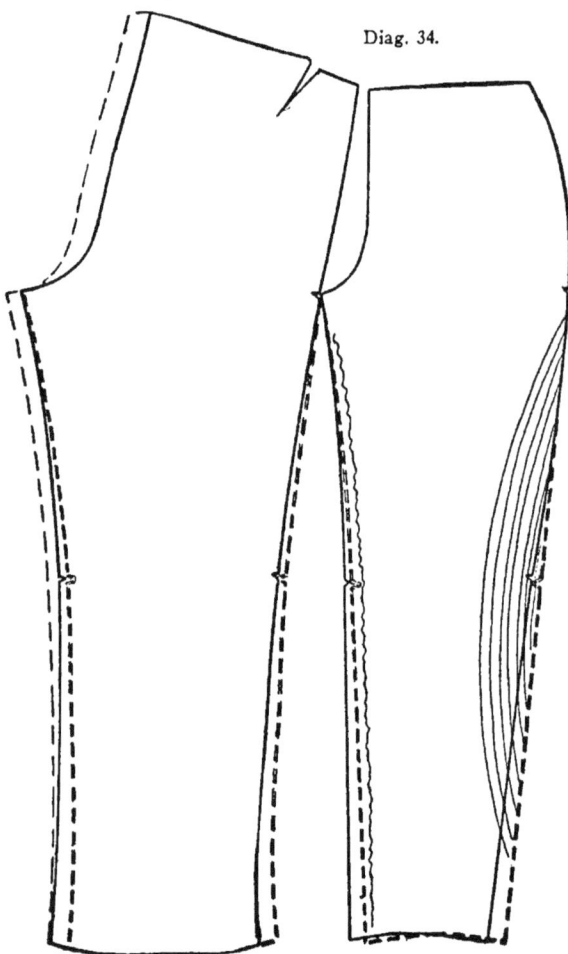

Diag. 34.

bottom to the hip and the material is to be thrown toward the inseam, but as no outlet is available on the forepart the outside seam edge must be stretched. The inseam is shrunk in until it falls as from the double, broken lines, which are the normal lines of the pattern as drafted, to the solid ones. On the backpart the outlet is utilized at the inseam and the same amount reduced at the outside seam, as from the broken to the solid lines.

The straightening of the back-center seam is often resorted to, but as the amount let out at the top must be taken off at the side seam there is no saving of work and, besides, there is no opportunity to have the forepart follow, and is, therefore, not as effective as the method just described.

ALTERATIONS ON TROUSERS

TOO TIGHT AT CROTCH.

Diagram 35 illustrates one of the most annoying faults in trousers; one that causes the wearer more discomfort than anything else. While it may be local in the crotch it is usually accompanied by tightness over the seat, across the part shown by the double arrow-head line. Even though they are of ample size at the side seam the fault may be emphasized at the center seam and the "cutting in" at that region makes the wearer feel as if he was gradually being cut in two.

The double, broken lines show the pattern as drafted and the single broken lines are the usual outlets. The heavy, solid lines show the alterations made, by adding more material across the seat and from the top of the inseam to the knee.

It goes without the saying that this re-shaping must be done carefully, since the run of these lines is as important as is the additional size. The size can be added without gaining the ease required, if the lines do not conform to the part of the body they are to fit. Size and outline must be given with the same object in view. The outline may undo the effect that the size properly given will otherwise produce.

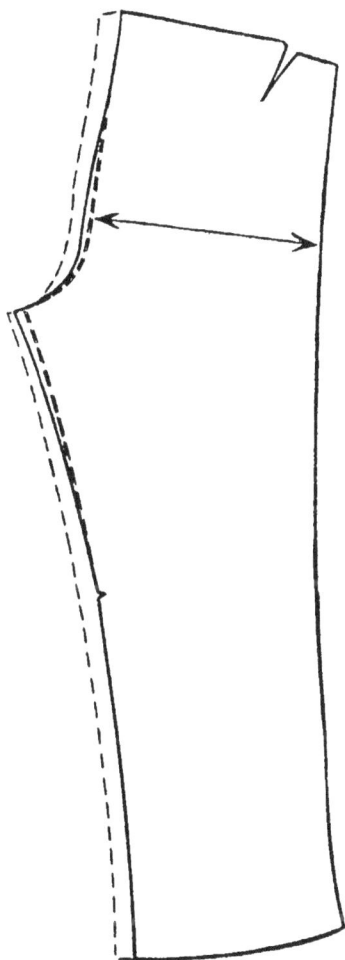

ALTERATIONS ON TROUSERS

FULLNESS BELOW THE SEAT.

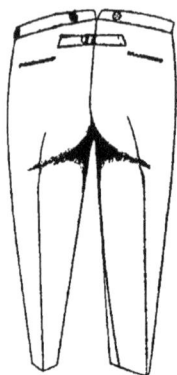

Diag. 36.

THIS fault is often one of wrong attitude. It is a fault most frequently found in trousers for erect men. This suggests that the original pattern has not been cut in keeping with the attitude of the man for whom they were cut.

Diagram 37 shows the remedy, and the surest way is to correct the pattern, take the trousers apart entirely and recut them. The pattern is corrected by cutting across both the backpart and the forepart and spread them at the front and overlap them at the back center seam, pivoting at the side seam, as illustrated. In emphasized cases it is well to deepen the back-center seam below the overlap, as by the circled lines.

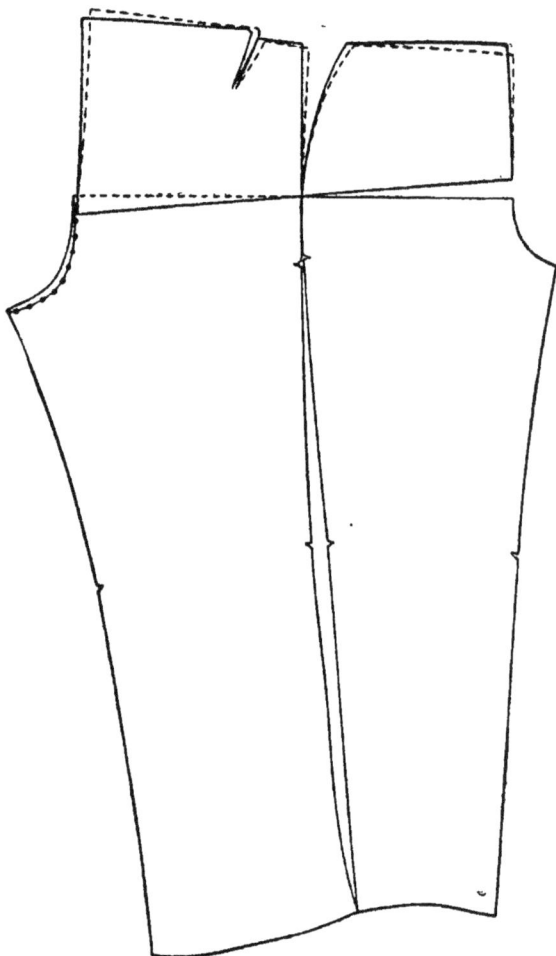

Diag. 37.

ALTERATIONS ON TROUSERS

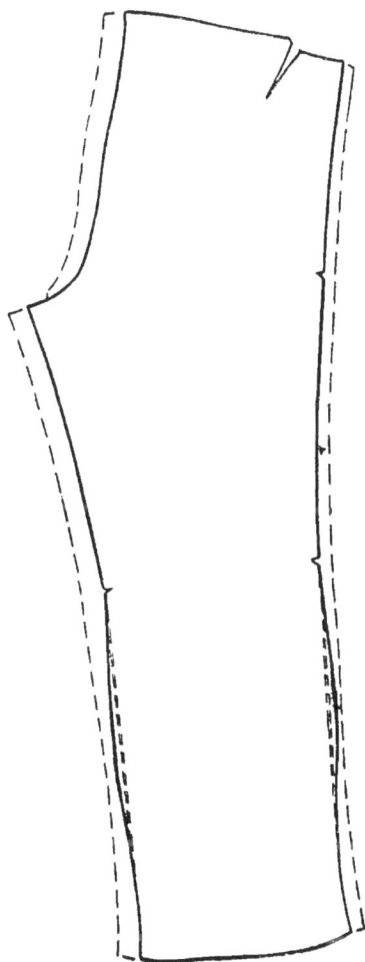

Diag. 38.

MANIPULATION FOR LARGE CALVES

Diagram 38 shows how to remedy trousers that strike on the ealf. This is particularly necessary when the calves are more than usually w e l l developed. Curve outward at both seams, as from the double, broken lines to the solid ones and press the rounding toward the center until the seams are straight. In general use care in shaping the parts before the seams are sewed.

The foregoing gives the principal alterations that come up every day in practice, which, if observed, not only gives the manner in which the faults should be remedied, but also suggests how to avoid them.

[Finis]

Milton Keynes UK
Ingram Content Group UK Ltd.
UKHW042050130824
446844UK00006B/332

9 781528 712583